Mind Games

Others Thoughts Inside of Me

INSPIRED BY HOLY SPIRIT
WRITTEN BY LONNEICE WEEKS-BADLEY

outskirtspress
DENVER, COLORADO

SPECIAL POEMS BY PERMISSION:
Secret...Secrets ....Rajahne Kymiece Smith-Dobbs
The Road To Life ....William S. Peters
Question in Answer Form ....Rodney Morine
Kiss Your Tears Away ....Chichina M. Smith
Deep Meditation...........................Oliver Renaldo Weeks

www.rajahnes.ghaw@yahoo.com
www.lonneice123@hotmail.com

Mind Games
Others Thoughts Inside Of Me

v3.0

ILLUSTRATIONS: COVER: Lonneice Weeks-Badley
COVER AND BACK PAGE DESIGNED: Outskirts Press
BOOK EDITOR: Outskirts Press

Outskirts Press, Inc.
http://www.outskirtspress.com

ISBN: 978-1-4327-9822-2

PRINTED IN THE UNITED STATES OF AMERICA

DEDICATED TO:

The Almighty GOD...

Who is and always will be the head of my life. It was He Who allowed me to write these wonderful works as the Holy Spirit inspired me to do so.
Thank You, Lord. All The Glory To You....

BATTERED WOMEN AND CHILDREN OF TODAY

Oliver Renaldo (Vego) Weeks
Dad, I miss you and will always keep you in my heart. I know that you're bringing laughter to the angels around you with your jokes. Dad, you left us your legacy – laughter and joy to all of us.
R.I.P. JULY 5, 1920 – JULY 31, 2010

Paul B. Anderson Sr.
Thank you for adopting us as your very own.
We love and miss you and will always keep you in our heart. We know that you're a guardian angel looking down on us.
R.I.P. SEPTEMBER 16, 1936 – NOVEMBER 22, 2010

ACKNOWLEDGMENTS

First and foremost God is the inspiration of my life. He's the rock that keeps me strong. He's my LOVING friend forever…

Bill Peters was persistent in encouraging me to use the gift that God has given me, to His Glory. I continue to hear his words: "Don't sit down on it. Share it!" I'm so grateful to have you as a friend. Thank you for helping me to refocus on my writings. ONE LOVE…

Mom, when I read a couple of my poems to you, your words were so touching to me. You loved "In My Doings," "I Want to Be Happy," and "Secrets…Secrets." Mom, you showed me how proud you were.

THANKS, MOM. I LOVE YOU…

To my dad Oliver R. Weeks for allowing me to use your poem "Deep Meditation." When you read that poem to me, tears came to my eyes as I realized that you're about to be 90 years of age, and you're so alert and full of fun. Thanks for the laughter… Dad got his wish, his 90th birthday party.

I LOVE AND MISS MY DAD

Thanks to my daughter Chichina Chishona M. Smith for allowing her daughter Rajahne to write her poem for this project, I also would like to thank Chichina (Shawn) for her poem "Kiss Your Tears Away."

I LOVE YOU, SHAWN…

Thanks a trillion to my granddaughter Rajahne Kymiece Smith-Dobbs for helping me to edit this work and for allowing me to use her gift to write "Secrets…Secrets" and to come up with the title "Writer's Block" in our first book… She's only fourteen years of age. You will see more of her work in the future.

I LOVE YOU, NAY NAY...

Rodney, I thank you for allowing us to use your poem "Question In Answer Form," which you recited at our family reunion in 2001. It's a pleasure to post your gift in this book. That was the first time I met you, and since then we have been very close.

LOVE YOU…ONE LOVE

Arlene P. Johnson, I definitely needed another pair of eyes. My gratitude and thanks to you for proofing my work.

LOVE YOU, MY DEAR FRIEND AND FORMER COWORKER

Thanks to all my former coworkers and friends from Verizon: Tarry Seward, Lorine Thomas, Brenda Durant Johnson, Audrey Wilson, Verge Harper, and Barbara Bass. Thanks to all my sisters and brothers in Christ: Evangelist Allie Layton, Deaconess Carrie King, Deacon and Deaconess Chris and Dawn Canady, Claudette Booker, Pastor Andru Kelly, and Inner-Core of One Church Worldwide Ministries for allowing me time off to complete this book. Each and every one of you showed me the confidence you had in me. All of you have extended love and encouragement and always told me to hang in there.

I have been truly inspired by your words of wisdom and support in my endeavor to write this book.

ONE LOVE=HIS LOVE FOREVER IN US TO ENCOURAGE AND SHARE WITH EACH OTHER IN LOVE DAILY... MAY GOD BLESS YOU ALL...

MIND GAMES
OTHERS THOUGHTS INSIDE OF ME

Contents

INTRODUCTION

Another day of rest. It feels good when you can meditate and hear from the Holy Spirit as to what He requires us to do. I love having quiet time with the Lord, as our conversation with each other gets sweeter every moment.

The start of another book—the Lord keeps giving them to me. However, I'm holding on to them until He informs me to publish them. I truly am impressed by what the Lord can do, and He has impressed me.

As a young child I suffered with convulsions in school, and I had a problem in reading, and comprehending what was just read. I was slow and could not spell, and in college I was afraid of how people or my professors would accept me.

In my Christian Bible classes I was afraid to let people look at my papers. My handwriting was awful, and still is! I was ashamed, and that's why my reports or whatever I need to write are typed. Thank the Lord for computers and keyboards! Now I can't get enough of reading and writing. Oh how I was blessed by the best.

Now as I write I'm inspired and directed under the authority of the Holy Spirit! He has used thoughts and doubts of what was really going on in the mind and put them in this book of poems called ***MIND GAMES***. The mind remembers everything you say and records the negative and the positive in the brain just like a tape recorder or computer.

There are those who react to the negative, which causes those crazy mind games.

HOW TO FIGHT THE BATTLE OF THE MIND

Each and every person has thoughts in their mind, and at times they will turn into a battle. But we must focus on God's way of living to fight this battle with HIS Word…

Hosea 4:6: "My people are destroyed for lack of knowledge."

Paul tells us time and time what to do to fight Satan's battle against our mind...

Ephesians 6:10-17: Be strong in the Lord and in the power of His might. Put on the *whole armor of God* that you may be able to stand against the wiles of the devil. For we do not wrestle against flesh and blood, but against principalities against powers against the rulers of the darkness of this age against spiritual hosts of wickedness in the *heavenly places*! Therefore take up the whole armor of God that you may be able to withstand in the evil day, and having done all, to stand. Stand therefore, having girded your waist with truth, having put on the *breastplate of righteousness,* and having shod your feet with the preparation of the gospel of peace; above all, taking the *shield of faith* with which you will be able to quench all the fiery darts of the wicked one. And take the helmet of salvation and the sword of the Spirit, which is the word of God.

It is Satan's job to put thoughts of evil intentions in our minds. They are negative images and insinuations which then become our thought patterns. Out of our own ignorance we allow him to control all aspects, actions, and thoughts of our mind… If Satan used his plans to try and destroy God first in Heaven, and then Adam and Eve on Earth, Jesus in the wilderness, and also HIS disciples as they went on their journey to win souls for Christ, what makes us (believers) exempt? God gave us all a mind of discernment of good and evil so that we can win this battle or conquer the mind games being played against our mind.

MIND GAMES
OTHERS THOUGHTS INSIDE OF ME

When you speak out loud what's on your mind

Are you opening up the mind's door

For spiritual warfare of the worst kind?

Satan comes ready for battle and to play the mind game with you

Others thoughts inside of me…

What could it be? Spiritual warfare of the worst kind is after me…

But I say to him, Oh no, not this time

This is a child of MINE

This time it's between you and ME...

These are Mind Games

Focus on ME, mind to mind

He can't hear you this time

Let ME know what's on your mind

I will hear you all the time
When we block him out
He will not win this bout
He will shoot his darts
But he will run out

He's ramping and raging as he pouts

And he's trying to figure this one out

As he roams about

Satan and his Mind Games will tremble and flee

'Cause she's now a part of ME

This time it's between him and ME

Let this mind that's in ME be in you as it is in ME

When you keep your mind on ME you will be set free

All you have to do is follow ME and agree

Philippians 2:4-6
5Let this mind be in you which was also in Christ Jesus,
6who, being in the form of God, did not consider it robbery
to be equal with God,

THE ROAD TO LIFE

the road we travel
may not be what we choose
but it does not mean
we have to lose
for all roads traveled
no matter the miles
have much to teach
in that road's trials
so keep your **mind** open
get out your pen and pad
record what you learn
the good and the bad
there will be challenges
with each twist and turn
for character's not given
character you earn
so never give in
though sometimes we may pause
but don't cheat yourself
and abandon your cause
for in time will come
your journey's end
your road will be straight
no curves nor a bend
the road of life
will teach us to see

how to use the gift

God gave you and me…life!

~ wsp ~

Project: "share the love"

SLEEPLESS NIGHTS

In my dark room as I tried to sleep

I tossed and turned throughout the night

My mind and I were having a fight

I guess it did not like what was in sight

It sure enough wasn't HIS light

Confusions of this...

Confusions of that...

All the things I saw, or watched on TV

Or the things I heard from people around me

All that was rattling in my mind

And caused it to disagree

It was just a figment of my imagination

That is why I have these sleepless nights

Turn over and meditate and enter into HIS rest...

HE will give you peace

So that you will sleep again

Sweet Dreams...

DRIFTING AWAY

Deep, deep in my sleep…
I felt as if I was Drifting Away…
Drifting Away…
I was floating and feeling that I was Drifting Away…
As I turned side to side in my sleep…
I felt as if I was Drifting Away…
How can I truly tell you what I was going through…
Unless you were there to see
What this thing could do to me...
You would be able to vouch for me...
There were times I thought I was dead…
You should have seen the vibrations of the bed…
And how I felt when I was Drifting Away…
Drifting Away…
The earthquake inside of me
Just woke me up from my sleep…
I felt as if I was Drifting Away
My body did shake, like an earthquake…
I felt I was Drifting Away…
My bed was shaking along with me…
It felt as if the earthquake
had just passed through me
Deep, deep in my sleep…
I felt as if I was Drifting Away…

Don't Drift Away…
Wake up, my child, it's me…

Next thing I knew, I was up on my feet…
Thank God, I'm alive and have been set free…

It's not time yet for you to drift away from me…
For this is my decree…
You have work on Earth to do for me…
I want you to pray…
For all those who have gone astray…
I want them all saved and set free…
Can you do that just for me…?

Now let me get off my feet and do His deed…

HE WOKE ME UP THIS MORNING

Yes! HE woke me up this morning

On HIS day HE had made

Oh how great it is that HE'S a friend of mine

And allowed me to be in HIS day one more time

HE heard me pray

For peace in my mind, throughout this day

Then HE blessed me

And then HE started me on my way

HE woke me up this morning

What a great day it will be...

For now HE'S in my mind guiding me...

STOP AND THINK

If only your heart had brains

Stop and think

Things wouldn't be this way

Stop and think

Your life would be better today

If you just rearranged your pathway

From the heart to the mind

Stop and think

If only your heart had brains

Things wouldn't be this way

Now it's time to rearrange

and you will see a great change

Once you change your heart

to think like your brain…

Stop and Think

THE BLINKING LIGHTS

When you see a blinking light do you know what it means?

Stop, don't move

Go, it's clear

Run, time's running out

Alert, keep focus

Yield, slow down

Warning, to save our life…

They are there to alert our mind and eyes

And to catch our attention

To protect us from the worst kind of intervention

Now keep your eyes on the prize, your mind will be set free

Of what is ahead of you and me

So you don't make a mistake and kill or hurt me

Even you, we know not which one it would be

So that you won't go through a life of pain and blame

For not following the rules of the blinking lights…

BUT IT'S OKAY

Inside our mind
Is an abundance of knowledge
It wants to transmit a message
but we won't let it...
But it's okay!
Trust in God! He will help you
He put it inside you to share
and to show them that you care...
Continue as He said
Give it to those who need to be fed...
I have problems...
But it's okay!
No matter what
Situation or circumstances
You or I may go through
He has our back
We all have flaws...
But it's okay!
He loves you...
He said that He would never
Leave us nor forsake us...
But it's okay!
He's our deliverer
He's our guard
He's our shield
He watches over everything
Just trust me!
But it's okay!

Remember My Word
Plant it in your mind
Plant it in your heart
Plant it in your soul…
He brings all things back to remembrance
Just call on Me!
But it's okay!
I'm already here
Inside your mind
To lead you all the way

MOVE OVER

Move Over
So that I can see
If there's room enough for me
Who are you?
Can't you see you can't get through?
My mind is filled with who I know.

Move Over
Who are you?

I'm just a new friend,
Hoping to be with you to your end
I want to be your new friend
Please let me in
There's no room in here for you
'Cause you are evil in all the things you do

Move Over
Who are you?

I don't need a friend like you
And that's the truth, it won't do
Oh yes! I'm talking to you
'Cause I don't know you.
I don't want you…
I don't hear you
And you're not in my mind…
Move…

CRACKING (MIND)

My mind is cracking

I don't know what's happening

It sends cracking signals

As it moves and wiggles and giggles

Up and down my head and neck

As I sit up or lie down in my bed

Doctors say that I'm stressing

But I know when Satan is messing

'Cause he's trying to steal

My God-given blessings

I need quiet time to rewind

Oh Lord, please restore my mind

You are a healer at all times

Thank you, Lord, now I feel fine

CRACKING MIND…

MIND OF FEAR

When will you let ME tap into your mind, my dear?
You have to let go of all the fear
I'm not the one who hurt you
I want to help you feel new
Your mind of fear is not allowing ME to get near
You showed ME that you care,
But your mind of fear is not allowing ME to get near
What must I do to get through to you?
I know you love ME as I do you
But your mind of fear is tearing us apart
God did not give you a spirit of fear
but of power, love and a sound mind
What must I do to get to you?
I don't want you to lose this fight
I don't want you to take a hike
I want to get into your mind and give you new light
I dream of you day and night
Am I losing you to this Mind of Fear?
Now look at ME
Can't you see
I want to live true to you
for the rest of your life, my dear

QUESTION IN ANSWER FORM

Why do the unknowing fear my blackness to death?

Why is death (the mysterious realm of the
unknowing) portrayed with blackness?
Listen to the unchained knowledge

Death is (as is the depth of my blackness) the
undeniable edge of the unknowing

Why do the unknowing fear death?

Because death is a point of knowledge which cannot
be understood without the ability to
perceive this knowledge

Why do the unknowing fear my blackness?

Because the blackness contains the unbridled
knowledge in its raw and most potent form.

This unknown knowledge contains the secrets
of life, encompassing death and keeping
the mysteries of life hidden beyond death

To my blackness, this knowledge is no secret

This is the question in answer form
Why is it a wonder that the unknowing
fear my blackness to death

By Rodney Morine (My Cousin)

SECRETS...SECRETS

DON'T STAY IN PLACE
SECRETS...SECRETS
HIT YOU IN THE FACE
THEY MAKE YOU CRY AND SCREAM AND SHOUT
THEY'LL KILL YOU, DESTROY YOU AND WON'T LET
YOU OUT
WHILE YOU CRY THEY KEEP ON ATTACKING
UNTIL THEY PULL OUT THE SPIRIT THEY'RE LACKING
THEY'LL KEEP YOU HIDING
IN THE TROUBLED SHAME
YOU YELL AT EVERYONE
WHEN YOU'RE THE ONE TO BLAME
SECRETS...SECRETS
HIT YOU IN THE FACE
SECRETS...SECRETS
DON'T STAY IN PLACE
SECRETS...SECRETS
ARE NOT FUN
SECRETS...SECRETS
HURT SOMEONE...

BY
RAJAHNE KYMIECE SMITH-DOBBS
MY GRANDDAUGHTER

LOST AND CONFUSED

I don't know which way I'm going
Because I'm lost and confused
I don't know if the LORD is calling me
I don't know if Satan is calling me
My mind is playing tricks on me
I don't know which way I'm going
Because I'm lost and confused
I hear a voice that says don't do that
I hear a voice that says it's all right
I hear these voices and I'm so confused
And don't know what to do
Get on your knees and pray for a mind of discernment
God is not the author of confusion, but of peace
If it's good things you're hearing
Then you know it's the LORD
If it's bad things you're hearing
Then you know not to do it
I do know which way I'm going
I'll choose the LORD'S

DO AS I SAY…AND NOT AS I DO

Look at me, Mama, I want to be just like you
We have the same outfit
And our hands on our hips too
My mind will hold this picture in its deepest depths
Mama, this is one picture I will never forget
As I grow older I want to be just like you
Oh no, daughter, I want you to be
A better person than me
DO AS I SAY…AND NOT AS I DO
But Mama, it's okay for you
I thought it was okay to step and walk in your shoes
I don't hear anyone scolding you
DO AS I SAY…AND NOT AS I DO
But Mama, I want to be just like you
Why can't I do as you do?
Mama, aren't I life to you
I lost my love now my life
I want to grow up as you do
My mind is messed up
My life is not right
I don't even have food to feed you at night
My baby, this is not right
I want you to have a better life
While your mind is bright
And full of HIS light
Do the things that will steer you right
DO AS I SAY…AND NOT AS I DO

TEARS OF A MOTHER...

MOTHERS ARE CRYING! THEIR KIDS ARE DYING!

YES! MY PEOPLE ARE (Destroyed) DYING FOR A LACK OF KNOWLEDGE!
OPEN YOUR EYES! COME OUT OF THAT DARK MINDSET! YOU ARE GOD'S CREATION AND YOU WERE BORN BLESSED!
USE THE WORD OF GOD TO WIN THIS FIGHT
TURN THE LIGHT ON! JESUS IS THE LIGHT!
HE WILL WIPE AWAY YOUR TEARS OF FRIGHT AND CARRY YOU THROUGH THE NIGHT!

STOP, MY SISTA! REMEMBER THIS…THE BATTLE'S NOT MINE BUT THE LORD'S! SAY IT! NO WEAPON FORMED AGAINST ME SHALL PROSPER!
TURN THE LIGHT ON, MY BROTHER! REMEMBER THIS! THE BATTLE'S NOT MINE BUT THE LORD'S! SAY IT! NO WEAPON FORMED AGAINST ME SHALL PROSPER!
OPEN YOUR MOUTH AND RENEW YOUR MIND! TELL THE DEVIL HE WILL NOT WIN THIS TIME…
PRESS FOR THE MARK, ENDURE TO THE END…

TURN YOUR LIGHT ON AND REMEMBER THIS:
MOTHERS WHO SOW TEARS SHALL REAP JOY
IN THE MORNING

RIVER OF TEARS/TEARS OF MY MIND

THE TEARS YOU SEE STARTED IN MY MIND
ARE FROM PAIN AND HURT OF THE WORST KIND
BUT THEY HAD TO COME OUT THROUGH MY EYES
MY MIND WAS FOGGED UP WITH PUDDLES OF TEARS
AND CAUSED A RIVER TO FLOW AND CAUSE MY FEARS
THEY HAD TO BE RELEASED FROM MY MIND
SO THAT I COULD THINK CLEARLY AT ALL TIMES
MY EYES ALREADY SAW WHAT WAS BUILDING IN ME
THEY SIGNALED MY MIND
AND SAID THEY WOULD SET ME FREE
FROM THIS RIVER OF TEARS
I THANK MY EYES FOR RESCUING ME
NOW I CAN THINK AND SEE
MY MIND HAS BEEN SET FREE…
FROM THE RIVER OF TEARS THAT WERE INSIDE OF ME…
TEARS OF MY MIND

BRAINWASHED

There's so much love inside you see
Brainwashed, is this really meant to be
Or is this just a game played against you and me

Brainwashed by the things you say to me…
Brainwashed by the things I say to you…
Brainwashed, how could this be so suddenly?

We don't even know each other, do we…
It's just one month! How could it be?

Brainwashed by your adorable looks
Brainwashed by your love talk
Brainwashed that we can't think these days…
Brainwashed, how could this be so suddenly?

You feel closed in…I feel closed out…

Brainwashed because we're not able to agree and see
These things we feel are lacking in you and me…

Communication and understanding, trust and openness
Fear of speaking and fear of doing…
Wondering if one would be hurt
because it was misunderstood…

A fear of loving with no love returned
Feelings of nothing but pain
If we just open up to each other in truth we both will gain…
Our fears are getting the best of us, can you agree?
We must let go of our fears,
and show how much we really care…

Brainwashed we're not, we're just in fear…
So let this fear set us free…
This love was set up; but not by you or me…
This was put together by a Higher Authority
We both said that we agreed,
Let our minds be free and in unity…
BRAINWASHED IS NOT WE…
ONE LOVE…HIS…IN US…

BECAUSE OF YOU

I DONE LOST MY MIND, AND GAVE IT TO YOU...

Now I have no life of my own because of you.
I DONE LOST MY MIND BECAUSE OF YOU...

You are controlling and I don't know what to do.
I DONE LOST MY MIND BECAUSE OF YOU...

There are days I'm happy and days I'm blue...
I have no life of my own because of you...
People confront me time after time and say,
This is not the person I once knew...
What happened to the love?
What happened to the time?
What happened to the friendship you had for others?

Can't you see, he's gotten you under dark covers...

I DONE LOST MY MIND BECAUSE OF YOU...

Now look at what you allowed him to do...
He took away your dignity and your value too...
Which were your treasure and virtues
Come from under those dark covers and be you...

You should not allow anyone to control you
and tell you what to do.

You had a mind of your own and it was so true
You're darn right! You lost your mind because of him…
It's time for me to restore my mind.
Bye, Bye, Baby
It's time for me to be me and not you…
This time it's not because of you…
It's because I'm a WOMAN OF VALUE AND PURPOSE…
Who God sets free is free indeed,
HIS DESTINY is my destiny…
DEDICATED TO ALL WOMEN WITH A LOW
SELF-ESTEEM…

SHAME

I was not in my right mind
When I met you
I was out there doing my do
With whomever would allow me to
I was truly going through the blues
I did not want it to hit the news
That's why I hid it from you
Now here you come and spoil my game
I married you and gave you my name
Despite the drugs, women and shame
You did not know, I hid it well
My destiny was heading straight to hell
I hoped that you did not see
The person I chose to be
A drug addict, yes that was me
I prayed to the Lord to set my mind free
But I couldn't get control of the enemy
There was a battle inside
Even I could not see his disguise
The drug that was taking control of my being
Baby, I'm sorry I put you to shame
I was not in my right frame of mind
When I met you
And gave you my name…SHAME

Kiss Your Tears Away

A Message from Our Creator

Tell **ME** one reason why you try to hide your tears inside
Can't you see **I'M** here for you,
regardless of what you may go through?
Give **ME** a chance to understand the situation that's at hand
No need for you to be alone, just call **ME**,
just pick up the phone

HOW LONG MUST I WAIT;
TO KISS YOUR TEARS AWAY?

You have to get this off your chest, holding it in isn't best
Since **I'VE** known you for some time,
allow **ME** to ease your MIND
You need **ME** more than anyone
I'LL be there till your tears are done
One day soon the pain will clear
It may leave tonight while **I'M** still here

HOW LONG MUST **I** WAIT TO KISS YOUR TEARS
AWAY?

I have always been here for you
I know your heart, and **I** know what to do
We've been friends all of your life
Each time you cried, **I** dried your eyes
So can **I** talk to you, for a little while?
I'M someone to make you smile

I tried so hard to be there for you, but you won't let **ME** in
to pick you up so that you can start all over again
Just call **ME** and let **ME** know what you need…
Just tell **ME**, don't let this drive you away from **ME**…
Just ask **ME**, since **I'M** here anyway…
AND JUST LET **ME** KISS YOUR TEARS AWAY

By
ChiChina Smith (My Daughter)

OVERTIME (PAST)

Lot's wife looked back one last time

She was destroyed for her frame of mind

Longing for her overtime

Will you stand there in the same frame of mind?

It's my time to let go of my overtime

But there's something in my mind

That won't let me leave it behind

Stop carrying me along with a negative frame of mind

When will you let go of your overtime

Don't you know it will destroy you in due time

It's a form of bondage that will blow your mind

Looking at your overtime

It's best to leave me behind

So that you can have a better life down the line

Overtime, overtime it's time to check out

'Cause this overtime has just run out

It's time to go home now with peace of mind

I'm saying goodbye for the very last time.

SATAN TRYING TO PULL ME DOWN

Satan trying to pull me down
But I'm not gonna let him win
He comes in your life
And he fills your mind with sin
Don't let him destroy your mind again
If you give in you won't make it to Heaven
I'm asking you all not to give in
Jesus is the one to choose
and you won't lose
Satan trying to pull me down
But he's not gonna win
Watch for that wicked frown
You will recognize this clown
He's the new guy in town
Satan trying to pull me down
But he's not gonna win

DARKNESS OF THE MIND

Why? Oh why, is it so dark?

Why is it tearing me apart?

Why is this breaking my heart?

This darkness of the mind

It is not kind

Please let my light turn on in time

Oh Lord, help me renew what was once fine

A mind with a bright light

That gave me peace throughout the night

This darkness of the mind it's not right

I know that I will win this fight

'Cause this light will shine so bright

And cast the darkness of the mind

Out of sight…

Oh how sweet it is to see this light again…

HE was there from the beginning…

HE is the light, which shines so bright…

Thank you, Lord, we won this fight…

MEDITATION OF THE MIND

CLOSE YOUR EYES FOR JUST ONE MOMENT
AND IMAGINE WHERE YOU WOULD LIKE TO BE
YOUR HOPES AND DREAMS CAN COME TRUE
NEGLECT NOT THE GIFT THAT IS IN THEE…
MEDITATE UPON THESE THINGS…
WHAT DO YOU SEE?
I IMAGINE MYSELF MAKING IT…
AND BECOMING WHAT I WANT TO BE…
A NEW LIFE WITH PEACE AND SERENITY…
I HAVE BEEN SET FREE FROM ME…
MY FEAR, MY HURTS, MY PAIN
WERE ALL BUT A GAME
CLOSE YOUR EYES FOR JUST ONE MOMENT
WHAT DO YOU SEE?
ME…STRIVING TO BE WHAT YOU WANT ME TO BE…
A BETTER PERSON INSIDE OF ME…
DON'T LET ANYONE TELL YOU ANY DIFFERENT…
'CAUSE YOU CAN BE WHAT YOU WANT TO BE
YOUR EYES HAVE BEEN CLOSED FOR SO LONG
NOW IT'S TIME TO OPEN YOUR EYES FOREVER…

SOMEONE UP THERE WHO CARES

I KNOW THAT THERE IS

SOMEONE UP THERE WHO KNOWS

WHEN YOUR MIND IS OUT OF CONTROL

SOMEONE UP THERE WHO CARES

WHAT WE'RE GOING THROUGH

SOMEONE WHO CARES IF WE LIVE OR DIE

SOMEONE WHO CARES AND CAN DRY OUR

WEEPING EYES

SOMEONE WHO CARES, WHO CARES FOR YOU

WHEN YOUR MIND IS OUT OF CONTROL

I AM…WHO LOVES ME AND YOU…

HE WILL FIX IT, JUST WAIT AND SEE…

HE'S THE ONE THAT CARES FOR YOU…

(A PROMISE)

I WOULD NEVER LEAVE THEE, NOR FORSAKE THEE

GOD IS WAITING

God is waiting, HE'S waiting for you
God is waiting for you
To make up your mind
Will you choose HIM?
There's not much time
HE wants to love you and give you life
Tap into your heart and mind
Set yourself free from you
So that we can be in perfect harmony
God is waiting, HE'S waiting for you
Just come and allow HIM to be your best
You will feel so much joy, peace and rest…
God, God is waiting
God, God is waiting
HE'S waiting for you

IN YOUR WAITING

While in your waiting allow patience to take place
as you wait patiently on me to set your mind free
from all that is inside thee.

Let the peace that surpasses all understanding work on your mind
and then allow it to saturate your heart.

Now allow the inner-being of the Holy Spirit to cleanse
your mind, heart and soul.

This new mind that you now have, let it stay focused on me.

I will set you free to the highest degree.

If you just trust in me, you will see
that the mind you once had
has been erased and made brand-new.
So that you can do what I ask of you!

My life I gave to you and that life it's so true because I love you and I know that you will follow through with what I ask of you.

So, my child, while in your waiting
I'm restoring you through and through.
Now this is the new person I made you.

There's nothing you or anyone else can do
because you are locked into me.

While in your waiting you have been set free…
To help others as I help thee…Amen

HE WANTS TO TAKE THE LEAD

Wait a little while longer so that there will be no delay
For His promises are much better at the end
Please, my beloved, just listen to me
God wants us to be happy and you'll see
That it's not about you, and it's not about me
It's about HIS LOVE that's embedded in our mind
Your mind is speaking of love and truth
You said you love me but in a different way
Be it for a day, His reason, or a season
Let's take this chance and see what happens
I said I love you, and it will be
In God's will and His way
I will obey and do as HE says
HE WANTS TO TAKE THE LEAD
Your heart, it doesn't know what to do
Your spirit is crushed because you're confused…
God doesn't give you a spirit of fear,
But of power, love and a sound mind
This is one love that's meant to be
HE WANTS TO TAKE THE LEAD
Now it's time to let go of your thoughts of doubt…
Rewind your mind and take your time
Or this love will never come about…

JUST TRUST ME

There are times that I regret
Allowing you to mess with my head
Days of disrespect and neglect
That's all that I knew how to accept
A love I thought that I had
Is no more, he has left me alone and torn
There are times I wish I was not born
I don't like this feeling of being alone
It may not be easy for me
To recognize he's not ready
But I'll come through it;
You just wait and see
My mind is not yet free from thee
My God will help me to be free
From all this hurt and misery
Not only in my mind but in my heart and soul
HE is the one that I must hold
Close to me to reach my goal
I heard HIM say
I know that it's not easy
To have your peace and live freely
But just trust ME,
This is not the way it was meant to be
But Just Trust ME

WRITER'S BLOCK

I have so much to write,

But my mind seems as if it has writer's block

And my hands are cramped

They won't even let me type a letter or two

It's as if my hands are stuck with glue…

I can't understand why I can't think

When there's so much inside of me to write with pen and ink

I don't want my time to run out

I'm on a time clock

Release my frustrations to peace

So that I can write a story that will give YOU glory

Help me get over this writer's block

My mind is filled with so much good stuff

But I must be released

Set my hands and mind free

So that I can write you the best story you would ever see…

WRITER'S BLOCK

My co-writer Rajahne Kymiece Smith-Dobbs

"MY DAY OF SOLITUDE"

I need this day of solitude
So that I can think with a clear mind
I need this day of solitude
So that I can recognize who's calling me
I need this day of solitude
So that I can hear your voice
I need this day of solitude
So that I can make the right choice
I need this day of solitude
So that I can have the peace that sets me free
I need this day of solitude
So that YOU can be with me
My day of solitude is with YOU, oh Lord
It feels so real, can YOU be on top of the hill
This is the day of my solitude
I feel the warmth, peace, joy and the love,
And this day I will never let go of…
MY DAY OF SOLITUDE

THE VISION

Write the vision and make it plain (Habakkuk 2:2)

It all starts in the mind...

The thoughts of what one must do...

When it is seen through the mind...

We must sit down and write it on paper this time

So we won't lose it, but use it

For a better life, down the line

Write the vision and make it plain...

So that you can start what will help you to gain

A better life, one full of prosperity

And hope and maybe fame

We must remember that an elephant never forgets...

But man will...and he regrets

That he did not write it down...

Write the vision and make it plain...

THE VISION

DEEP MEDITATION (From a Soldier)

This is my moment of deep meditation

Just thinking and yearning
And longing for you

But why did this have to start (war)
When you were so close to my heart

I know I'm lonely because of you

But I'll keep remembering
Until my dreams come true

This is a poem from a soldier's heart for his first love (1942)

MY DAD...

WHO ARE THEY?

Who are they to proclaim what is in your mind
Who are they to say that you are not doing fine
PSYCHOLOGIST/PSYCHIATRIST
Don't they understand that you're a child of MINE
They are there only for the money and fame
They need to stop playing these funny games
'Cause your mind is not insane
You're just hurting from others who caused you so much pain
Yes! It stayed in your mind
And caused you to feel worse at times
Release the hurt, release the pain
Don't hold on to the shame
You're MY child with a wonderful name
Just call on ME
I have no shame
To tell you that these doctors are playing games
You have been released from the toxic darkness of the mind.
WHO ARE THEY?
Ordinary people trying to read your mind...

I STILL SEE IT "BUT NOT WITH MY EYES"

I still see it, but not with my eyes
I see it in my mind
I saw how you were unkind
To people all the time

I still see it, but not with my eyes
I see it in my mind

How can I remove this hurt and anger of mine,
Which is deeply rooted in my mind?

I still see it, but not with my eyes
I see it in my mind

I will learn to forgive
So that my mind can live

I still see it, but not with my eyes
I see it in my mind

Will my mind have peace without disease?

I still see it, but not with my eyes
I see it in my mind

Now it's time for me to release
What I see in my mind
So that I can be free and feeling fine

I still see it, but not with my eyes
I see it in my mind

Will you forgive me this time
So that I can erase it from my mind
And be set free with no crime

I feel it in my mind…I'm free…

IN MY DOINGS: "I WANT TO BE HAPPY"

In my doings, I want to be happy…
How can I be
When I can't be me?
Who can I be
When I'm not free?
'Cause the inside of my mind is unhappy…

In my doings, I want to be happy…

When I do for others…
It releases my covers…
Covers of guilt, hurt, pain and shame…
Covers that play no games…
Covers that hold no blame…
Lord, as you teach me now how to see
What was truly hidden inside of me
In my doing for others I realized my inner weaknesses

In my doings, I want to be happy…

A lover of God with no covers…
Happy in love with you, Lord…
Happy in love with myself…
Happy in love with others…
Help me, Lord, to remove my covers…

In my doings, I want to be happy…

Lord! Take away the guilt…
Lord! Take away the hurt…
Lord! Take away the pain…
Lord! Take away the shame…
Lord! No more games…
And no more blame…
Lord! Help me to regain my name…

In my doings, I want to be happy…

So that it can show me and others…
What I have discovered
From under my covers
In my doings, I found The Real Me…

LEAVING IT UP TO YOU, LORD

I'm calling on YOU, LORD
YOU said to call on YOU
No matter what our mind may go through
I'm leaving it up to YOU, LORD
Because YOU know what to do
I'm calling on YOU, LORD
I'm down on bended knees
And requesting YOUR release
I'm calling on YOU, LORD
YOU'RE my light, my sunshine,
And the breeze that comes from the trees
YOU'RE the air that I breathe
YOU'RE always there for me
I know YOU'LL set me free
Once I release myself to thee
I'm leaving it up to YOU, LORD
Because YOU know what to do
I'm calling on YOU, LORD
Thank YOU, LORD
You set me free from the inner depth of me
For I was my worst enemy

THE TINY SEED (LOVE)

My mind was free and empty
Until that SEED entered into me
It started out so small
But look at how it has grown
How can something in my mind that was so minute
Grow to be so big?
I thought it was just a headache
But it would not go away
It keeps on throbbing in my mind
As it grew in time
This is a seed of TRUE LOVE,
And your mind is about to explode
Because you did not recognize this tiny seed
When it manifested in that deep hole
To show you how LOVE starts to grow
Now that you know about this tiny seed,
And know that it came from above
It's time to share your love with others…

THE TINY SEED (LOVE)

CAREFREE MINDS

Why are children's minds so carefree

When they're born as sweet as they can be

Loving babies, do you agree?

They have no fear until they became alert to see

Their surroundings, which are so bleak

They only copy what they hear and then they speak

Who put it in them—was it you, was it me

Or was it just the work of the adversary?

God does not give us a spirit of fear

But of power, love and a sound mind

Let us get our mind back as a little baby...

One that's carefree...

CAREFREE MINDS...

WHAT HAPPENED TO THE RAIN

It was pouring as hard as it could, you see
WHAT HAPPENED TO THE RAIN
It's raining down, cats and dogs
That was a saying old folks would say
And for me, it did not go away
WHAT HAPPENED TO THE RAIN
The child with this curious and inquisitive mind
Began to wonder, What if
I ask God for a new friend
One I could keep forever and to the end?
The rain was pouring as she played
But she had her rain gear on
It kept her from getting drained
Then she closed her eyes and focused in her mind
And began to pray for a friend of a different kind
WHAT HAPPENED TO THE RAIN

The rain started to subside

Then she saw a small puddle along the side

Something tiny crawling on its backside

So she went to see what it could be

IT WAS A FROG!

"That's what I asked of thee

Thank you, Lord, for sending it to me

Let me see if it is fine

It's alive and this is the new friend of mine"

Ask anything of HIM, and you shall RECEIVE

If you just BELIEVE

WHAT HAPPENED TO THE RAIN

FOCUS

How can I focus
When my mind is in disarray?
How can I focus
When I can't think of what to say?
How can I focus
When my mind has gone astray?
How can I focus
When my energy is not of God's Way?
How can I focus
When my perspectives are foggy and gray?
How can I focus
When my mind can't see from day to day?
How can I focus
When my perspectives are not as clear
As you want them to be?
How can I focus
When I can't show you the true me?
How can I focus
When you don't recognize it's all about you
And what you want to do?
How can I focus
When my mind thinks and is stayed only on your views?
How can I focus
When it's all about you?
Lord, set my mind free from him…
So that we both can clearly see
Let our focus be about HIM and not about you or me
Where's Your Focus?

RESPONSIBILITY

Whose responsibility is it?
Is it mine, is it yours…

If you respond to your thoughts
You may be wrong or you may be right…
Choose the ONE that will enhance your life…
The one that will LOVE you until the end…

It's your responsibility to choose what's right

Your mind may say that it's not for you
Your mind might say okay let's do
You just don't get this…

You must choose what's best for you…

It's your RESPONSIBILITY…

What do I have to choose…
Choose what's right…
So that your mind will be free
and you'll have a brighter life…
The ONE is ME…

I'M SORRY

I COME TO YOU, LORD, TODAY
I COME TO YOU, LORD, TO PRAY
I COME TO YOU, LORD, TO SAY
THAT I'M SORRY, SO SORRY
I SINNED AND SHAMED THEE
WHEN I KNEW THAT YOU LIVED IN ME
PLEASE, LORD, HELP ME…SET ME FREE
HELP ME CLEAR MY MIND
I COME TO YOU, LORD, TO SAY
THAT I'M SORRY, SO SORRY
PLEASE FORGIVE ME AND HELP ME…SET ME FREE
FROM THIS MISERY I ALLOWED TO COME UPON ME
WHILE YOU LIVED INSIDE OF ME
I'M SORRY, SO SORRY, PLEASE FORGIVE ME
I COME TO YOU, LORD, TODAY
I COME TO YOU, LORD, TO PRAY
I COME TO YOU, LORD, TO SAY
THAT I'M SORRY, PLEASE FORGIVE ME

ABBA FATHER, I LOVE YOU...

ABBA FATHER, I LOVE YOU

YOU'RE ALWAYS ON MY MIND

ABBA FATHER, I LOVE YOU

FOR THE GREAT THINGS YOU HAVE DONE

ABBA FATHER, I LOVE YOU

YOUR VICTORY IS WON

BECAUSE YOUR ONLY BEGOTTEN SON

JESUS GAVE HIS LIFE FOR ME

AND REQUESTED THE HOLY SPIRIT

TO LIVE INSIDE OF ME...

I HAVE BEEN SET FREE...

ABBA FATHER, I LOVE YOU...

YOU'RE THE AIR THAT I BREATHE

I wake up in the morning feeling free

Is it because I spent the night with thee

YOU'RE THE AIR THAT I BREATHE

As I take a deep breath

I feel YOU in me

YOU'RE THE AIR THAT I BREATHE

My mind has been set free

With my eyes closed

I vision and I feel a newness flowing through me

My hands are shaking, and my feet are tingling

My mind is as clear as can be

Just filled with YOU and me

YOU'RE THE AIR THAT I BREATHE

FATHER'S PRETTY LITTLE GIRL

YOU'RE ONE FILLED WITH LOVE AND JOY JUST LIKE ME
YOU'RE AS PRETTY AS CAN BE
LIKE A ROSE PLUCKED FROM ITS TREE
ONE THAT GLOWS LIKE THE RAINBOW
AND COLORFUL AS A FREE BUTTERFLY
DON'T LET YOUR MIND TAKE IT AWAY
WHEN YOU HEAR NEGATIVE THINGS
SOME PEOPLE MAY SAY

FATHER'S PRETTY LITTLE GIRL

KEEP YOUR MIND ALERT
I DON'T WANT YOU TO BE HURT
I CREATED YOU IN **MY** IMAGE
WITH LOVE, LIFE AND BEAUTIFUL COLORS
FOCUS ON THE ENERGY
OF THE COLORS OF YOUR MIND
LIVE ON, MY CHILD
YOU WILL BE JUST FINE…
FATHER'S PRETTY LITTLE GIRL

INSIDE ALL THREE

MY HEART, MY MIND, MY SOUL
THEY ALL BELONG TO YOU
MY HEART, MY MIND, MY SOUL
ARE INSIDE OF ME BECAUSE YOU
CREATED IT TO BE
MY HEART, MY MIND, MY SOUL
THEY'RE ALL ONE
AND THAT'S YOU
PLANTED INSIDE OF THIS BODY
INSIDE ALL THREE
MY HEART, MY MIND, MY SOUL
THEY ALL BELONG TO YOU

JUST A LITTLE LOVE

Just a little love
More love, more love
More love, from our people
Free your mind
Hold on to the little love
That you have in your mind and heart
And take it a very long way
Do as GOD asks you
Take your love, give it out
To those who need a new mindset
Help them! Fill them with your love
Take your love; it came from above
Give it out as you yell and shout
How this wonderful love came about
To those who need your love and are in doubt
Just a little love
Your little love will be a lot because it's ME
They will receive

MY VISION OF HOME

WHILE I SIT AND MEDITATE AND WAIT FOR YOU
I ENVISION A HOME
WHERE THE SKIES ARE EVER BRIGHT
A HOME OF JOY, PEACE AND LOVE DIRECTED BY YOU
I ENVISION A HOME
A HOME WHERE MANSIONS ARE NOT BUILT WITH HANDS
ANGELS ARE FLYING AROUND THE THRONE DAY AND NIGHT
THERE ARE NO MORE TEARS
'CAUSE GOD WIPED THEM AND GAVE YOU NEW EYESIGHT
NO DEATH NOR SORROW NOR CRYING NOR PAIN NOR HATE
IN THIS VISION OF HOME
NOTHING BUT LAUGHTER AND HAPPY SONGS
OH LORD! HOW I WAIT AND MEDITATE! WAIT TO GO HOME
I ENVISION YOU COMING TO TAKE ME ALONG
TO THIS PLACE CALLED THE NEW EARTH OR NEW HEAVEN
WHERE EVERYONE SHOWS LOVE AND IS AS ONE
WILL IT BE MY NEW HOME
OKAY. I'LL WAIT FOR YOU
MY VISION OF HOME

I'M SO THANKFUL TO YOU, LORD

Enter into His gates with thanksgiving,
and into His courts with praise!
Be **thankful** to Him,
and bless His name. **Psalm 100:4**

I'm so thankful to you, Lord, for changing me

You brought me from a mighty long way

And this is why I come to say

I'm so thankful to you, Lord, for changing me

I used to hang out in the clubs

I used to drink and get drunk and it wasn't good

My mind was confused and bombed out

I did not know my where's and my bout's

If it wasn't for You, Lord

I couldn't have known just where I'd be

You brought me from a mighty long way

If it wasn't for You, Lord

Today I'd probably be running astray

I'm so thankful to You, Lord

For coming my way

I'm so thankful to You, Lord, for changing me

MANIFEST THE JOY

Manifest the JOY

The JOY that lives in your mind

Manifest the JOY

The JOY that lives in your heart

Manifest the JOY

The JOY that lives deep in your soul

'Cause the JOY is the LORD

He's worthy to be praised

HOLD MY HAND

Hold my hand and guide me
To the PROMISED LAND
Don't let it go

Hold my hand until my mind can understand
That this is God's Son holding my hand
Hold it until I know my MASTER'S plan
Hold my hand as if it were YOUR very own
Don't let it go

If I lose YOUR hand I might be troubled
So don't let
Don't let it go

I recall You saying that You would never
Leave me nor forsake me
Hold MY HAND, O LORD

Until we get to the PROMISED LAND
HOLD MY HAND

I'M GOING HOME

I'M GOING HOME TO SEE
THE ONE WHO WAITS FOR ME
I'M GOING HOME TO SEE MY LORD

YOU TOLD ME THAT THERE'LL BE
A BETTER PLACE JUST FOR ME
I'M GOING HOME TO SEE MY LORD

I KNOW I TRIED TO BE EXACTLY
LIKE YOU WANTED ME TO BE
THERE HAVE BEEN TIMES I ALLOWED
SATAN TO COME AGAINST AND TRY TO RUIN ME
I HAD MORE FAITH AND TRUST
IN YOU, MY LORD

I'M GOING HOME TO SEE
THE ONE WHO WAITS FOR ME
I'M GOING HOME TO SEE MY LORD

I HAVE A QUESTION
ONLY YOU CAN ANSWER FOR ME
SOMETIMES I WONDER…
WAS MY MIND REALLY SET FREE

YOU MADE IT HERE
TO ME, MY CHILD…
AND THAT IS ALL THAT MATTERS TO ME
YOU HAVE BEEN SET FREE…

I'M HOME WHERE I SHOULD BE
I'M GOING HOME

PEACE AND MORE PEACE

PEACE I GIVE TO YOU

PEACE THAT SURPASSES ALL UNDERSTANDING

DWELLS WITHIN YOU

PEACE THAT SETS YOUR MIND FREE

SO THAT YOU CAN RELATE WITH ME

PEACE I GAVE TO YOU

PEACE FOR YOU TO GROW IN

PEACE FOR YOU TO ENJOY AND LOVE

NOW BE WHO I CALLED YOU TO BE

PEACE OF MIND WITH YOU AND ME

GOD'S ANGELS WITH THE COLORS OF A RAINBOW

The colors of a rainbow
How sweet they look on God's angels

Oh what bright and beautiful colors
Are they also beautiful to others

What kind of mindset did you discover
They are GOD'S angels with no hidden covers
and they are set free
And here's another thing I see
LOVE, JOY, HAPPINESS, and PEACE

WOW...This is just for me

Yes. For you and all GOD'S children
From the BEGINNING TO THE END
Can't you see that these angels are FREE
Praying for you and me
So that we can all agree?

That GOD'S people are in unity in their mind
No matter the race or the face
This mind and face show no hate
If they do, it's time to erase
The colors in your mind
Would have to take their place
There'll be no time to waste
Remove the disgrace
And shame from your face

God's not allowing it to come
Into HIS Heavenly place
These are the colors of HIS LOVE and GRACE

WHEREVER THERE'S LOVE THERE'S PEACE

There will be peace in the Valley of the LORD

Up in here there's love and peace

and all you need

Come on and follow me

So that you can see

All minds are set free

WHEREVER THERE'S LOVE THERE'S PEACE

Let HIM be the one that will release

You from old deeds

God shall **supply** all your needs
according to His riches in glory by Christ Jesus
Philippians 4:19

'Cause He is the one that created everything
He is our LOVE & PEACE IN EVERYTHING

NEW MOOD BLUE

The beautiful blue skies are looking down on you…
Why are you so blue?
The color blue is so moody, will it change my mood?
No, my child, this color blue is especially for you...
This is what I call the new mood blue…
Let it calm and soothe your mind
It will change in due time…
Let me treat you like no other can do
ONENESS…it's been searching for you
to be inside your mind, heart and soul…
Is not that your goal?
Oh my! What's happening to my mind?
It's being refreshed with MY LOVE…
This kind of LOVE you will never get from earthly lovers
It is unconditional LOVE, I give it to you forever…
Just close your eyes and let go and let it be
Let me dance your hurts, pains, and your shame away
Focus on ME as we dance in this LOVE and we sway…
It's ME and you
I want your mind to feel brand-new
Can you see what the color blue can do?
LORD…LORD…LORD…
It's YOU that I loved all the time
Oh! How could I have been so blind
almost lost my mind
for love…but what love…
It wasn't YOUR LOVE I felt
LORD, I realized that I'm in love with YOU
LORD, can I have this dance with YOU tonight?
My mind is feeling this great delight…
I want to feel the blue skies and your LOVE enter into me

It's MY light and I want to draw you closer and closer
After this dance there will be no other
Now your mind, heart, soul and MY LOVE
have connected together forever…
My child, this will not be your last dance…
Trust ME and come out of your trance…
What a wonderful view of the blue skies
You and ME, we're both dressed in blue…

RESCUED BY HIS LOVE

MY MIND WAS RESCUED BY HIS LOVE
A BLESSED LOVE FROM ABOVE
MY MIND WAS RESCUED BY HIS LOVE
HIS LOVE CAN SAVE YOUR MIND FROM YOU
AND THESE ARE THINGS HE'S PLEASED TO DO
HE COMES IN YOUR HEART AND YOUR MIND
HE CALMS YOU DOWN AND THAT IS FINE
I'M RESCUED BY HIS LOVE
HE COMES IN YOUR HEART AND YOUR MIND
HE TURNS YOU AROUND ALL THE TIME
AND ALL OF A SUDDEN YOU CLOSE YOUR MIND
BUT REMEMBER I'M
RESCUED BY HIS LOVE…ALL THE TIME…

I SURRENDER ALL

I REACH UP TO HIM,
EVERY NOW AND THEN
KNOWING THAT HE WILL BE MY FRIEND
AS I SURRENDER MYSELF ONLY TO HIM
ALL TO MY BLESSED SAVIOR
I SURRENDER ALL OF ME
EVEN TO THE BOTTOM OF MY FEET
AT TIMES IT IS PERSONAL AND INTIMATE YOU SEE
AS HIS LOVE GETS DEEPER INSIDE OF ME
I FEEL MYSELF IN LOVE AND FREE
'CAUSE THIS IS A TRUE RELATIONSHIP
BETWEEN HIM AND ME
THAT'S WHAT HE WANTS IT TO BE
HIS LOVE HAS TRULY CAPTURED ME
HIS EYE IS ON THE SPARROW
AND I KNOW THAT HE WATCHES OVER ME
HE KEEPS ME ALERT AND SETS ME FREE
FROM DANGERS SEEN AND UNSEEN
DO YOU KNOW WHAT I MEAN?

FAVORITE POEMS & NOTE SPACE

MIND GAMES
SCRIPTURE VERSES

SCRIPTURE VERSES

I Corinthians 14:33 (Lost And Confused)
For God is not the author of confusion, but of peace.

Deuteronomy 31:8 (Someone Up There Who Cares)
He would never fail thee, nor forsake thee.

Ephesians 6:10-13 (Satan Trying To Pull Me Down)
Be strong in the Lord and in the power of His might. Put on the whole armor of God that you may be able to stand against the wiles of the devil. For we do not wrestle against flesh and blood, but against principalities, against powers, against the rulers of the darkness of this age, against spiritual host of wickedness in the heavenly place. Therefore take up the whole armor of God that you may be able to withstand in the evil day, and having done all, to stand.

Hebrew 13:5 (Someone Out There Who Cares)
(A Promise) I will never leave thee, nor forsake thee.

Hosea 4:6 (Writer's Block) (Tears of a Mother)
"My people are destroyed for lack of knowledge."

James 1:8 (Responsibility)
A double minded man is unstable in all his ways.

Philippians 2:5-6 (Mind Games)
Let this mind be in you which was also in Christ Jesus, who, being in the form of God, did not consider it robbery to be equal with God.

Philippians 4:19 (Wherever There's Love There's Peace)
God shall **supply** all your needs according to His riches in glory by Christ Jesus.

Proverbs 3:5-6 (Just Trust Me)
Trust in the Lord with all thy heart and lean not unto your own understanding. In all thy ways acknowledge him, and he shall direct thy path.

Psalms 126: 5 (Tears of a Mother)
They that sow in tears shall reap in joy.

1 Timothy 4: 14A 15A
Neglect not the gift that is in thee…Meditate upon these things…

2 Timothy 1:7 (Mind of Fear)
God hath not given us the spirit of fear; but of power, love, and a sound mind.

Psalm 100:4 (I'M SO THANKFUL TO YOU, LORD)
Enter into His gates with thanksgiving, and into His courts with praise! Be thankful to Him, and bless His name.

FACEBOOK
FRIENDS
&
FAMILY
THOUGHTS AND COMMENTS

THOUGHTS & COMMENTS

To all my Facebook friends who commented on the five poems posted for you all to view. I was overwhelmed with the responses I received. Your encouragement helped me to continue in the gift that God has given me and to show to you all. These are just a few of my FBF who commented on my profile…

Mary Alexander-Hartsfield
Wow! How awesome!!! **GOD'S ANGELS WITH THE COLORS OF A RAINBOW**

Lord Xodus
Yes Lonneice keep blessing the peace, please.

Allie Layton
Lonneice, keep doing GOD's will, this is just the first step to where He is going to take you! OH yeah, there is so much more from here!!! I love it!

William S. Peters Sr.
Keep on writing sis.

Mike Turner
Hey Sis,
I like this! I too write poems, they have open mike at the Firehouse Cafe. Let me know if you would like to go!

Malachi Lane
Beautiful

Beverly A. McKenzie
Thank you for sharing one of God's greatest gifts, to mankind. Which is expression of creativity? And we who have

been blessed to do so, come into the realm of creation. It is our closest kinship to who he is. God who created the heavens and the earth! How blessed are we... That he blessed us with such a wonderful gift that displays him through our expression of praise! Continue to inspire us, as we give praise to him for you. God bless!

Brenda Durant Johnson
Lonneice, This is awesome. You are truly using the gift that our Heavenly Father has anointed you with. Keep it strong for JESUS!!!!!!!!!!!!!!

Fenese Carter, Roxanne London
Like This…

Allie Layton
THAT IS SO NICE, I HOPE THAT FROM READING YOUR WRITING SOME MOMMAS WILL GET THE RIGHT MESSAGE, **'DO AS I SAY...AND NOT AS I DO!'** VERY, VERY GOOD!!!

Adelle Banks-Wilson
That is really nice Lonneice. Thanks so much for sharing!!!

William S. Peters Sr.
Very nice write . . .

Scott Newman
Very talented...I do not share your gift Lonneice. The best I can do is, "roses are red, violets are blue..."....LOL

Christopher H Canady
I FINALLY READ IT. I LIKE IT.

Thurselle Chisolm-Watts
Amen Momma Lonni- Keep writing

Allie Layton

MY FAVORITE **NEW MOOD BLUE**, THE LOVE OF GOD SO BEAUTIFUL AND SO TRUE! THAT'S WHY I AM SO IN LOVE WITH HIM, BECAUSE HIS LOVE COMPARES TO NO MAN!!! THAT INNER LOVE, OH, MY, THANK YOU JESUS! AND I THANK GOD FOR YOUR ANOINTING IN YOUR WRITINGS, VERY UNIQUE, MY SISTER!!! LOVE YOU

Ani Blue

Oh! Beautiful Lonneice!! What a wonderous tribute to the growth of your inner visionary state that embraces the satisfying l.o.v.e. & wonder of Blue!!!!♥ ♥ ♥ ♥

Mary Alexander-Hartsfield

Beautiful!!! you are soooo anointed my Sister! God Bless you!

Mike Turner

AMEN!! Sister this is heart felt.

Deborah Stafford-Foushee

Hallelujah, this is sooo beautiful, love it.

Allie Layton

BEAUTIFUL!!! **What happened to the Rain…?**

Tenoa Anderson

I got all 5 they r so nice

Ani Blue

William S. Peters Sr.

(~;

Fenese Carter,

Like This…

Janice Dobbs
Thank you! Lonneice. I enjoyed talking to you last evening. I really enjoyed reading the poems in your book. I haven't finished yet. Looking forward to purchasing your book when it is published.

All those who like "I Surrender All"
Roderic Sells Twyman, Keyva Luvindanume Jones, LaShawnda Manson, Lucy Rivera, Darlene Mike-White, Donna Durant, Apostle Marcellus Sneed, Barry Wiseman Gloria Angela Davis

Allie Layton
Your writing is so true, He completes me in every way possible! And you feel free, He holds you in His arms and do not let go! He also watches over you, keeping you away from danger, with warnings from dreams or His voice! Letting me know that I am His own!!! **I Surrender All**

Jody Hooks
Thank u sista, n my times of trial and trivia, ur uplifting words are very appreciated. Thank you, besides being able to say good mornin, ain't nothin better than wakin up to Gods blessings.

Fenese Carter,
Like This…

Mind Games "Others Thoughts Inside of Me" All those who responded with like: Nicole Taylor, Pamela Martin Cotton, Helen Batucan-Ratz, Vanessa Rutherford, Latonya Pharr Archie, Rece Hairston, Gerald Curry, PhantasyCleveland Prez, Mercy J Abbah

Mary Alexander-Hartsfield Awesome! ♥

Eric L. Burt - Inside the Soul of Me Excellent write... The mind is the devil's workshop and an idle one definitely opens up the door to satan's mind games... But if we keep our mind and thoughts on Him, then like your poem says, "satan and his mind games will tremble and flee"... I'm truly glad you shared this write with myself and the other readers... God Bless you and your upcoming book as well as everything you put your hand too... Guidance & Protection... One Love...!!!

Norma Weathersby This write is very mesmerizing!! I think everyone can identify with it because the enemy walks to and fro thinking about who he is going to devour. So he will always try to come after us at some point in our life. As you said, "stay focus on the Lord" and the enemy will not achieve his goal. Remaining focus is just like wearing the whole armor of God and you will always have his protection. I was truly blessed by this write and may the Heavenly Father continue to anoint you to keep blessing us with your craft!!

Norma Weathersby @Eric I am in total agreement with every word you said....I cant wait to see more from this author!

Eric L. Burt - Inside the Soul of Me @ Norma - This is an AWESOME write here and I too am looking forward to reading more from the author... And if the book is anything like this write then all who purchase it will be in for a Holy Spirit Awakening... lol

Norma Weathersby @Eric, I agree once again. Seems like it will be just what the Lord ordained because we all tend to lose focus sometimes. I know I do so I will be keeping a watchful eye on when the book hits the web or bookstores. I have a hobby of downloading books now but either way you can't go wrong.

Thank you so very much FBF & family. I'm honored by your words of encouragement.

ONE LOVE…

May God Rain Down His Blessings
On Each and Every One of You!

ABOUT THE AUTHOR:

God is the LOVE of my life and I serve HIM with all my heart and soul. I AM SOLDED OUT FOR HIS LOVE, WHICH DWELLS INSIDE OF ME.

I, Lonneice Weeks-Badley, was born on November 6, to Oliver and Margaret in Harlem Hospital, Manhattan, New York, and now I reside in Edison, New Jersey. I am the mother of two daughters, Kimbelyn Smith-Campbell and Chichina M. Smith, proud grandmother of three grandsons, Rahjon (RahRah), Shaquan, and Jamir, my sweet, loving, and only granddaughter, Rajahne (Nay Nay) (Rah Rah named her), and one great granddaughter, Alannah.

Graduated from Essex College of Business as an executive secretary and also attended Essex County College for Business Administration.

I attended New Hope Baptist Church in Newark, New Jersey, and worked with the Prison Outreach and Food and Clothing Ministry. My tutorial to become a minister came from the Overseer Pastor Joe A. Carter. My first trial sermon was January 7th, 2004 and I was accepted as an associate minister by Pastor Carter, the Deacon/Deaconess Board, and the church family until my season was up.

I am presently retired from Verizon Telephone Company. I gave them 29 years of my time.

My time is dedicated to the Lord's work. I enjoyed my season working with the Timothy Evangelism Ministry – overseen by

Pastor Nick Smith and Minister Mary Hodges and all covered under the Overseer Bishop David G. Evans at Bethany Baptist Church, located in Lindenwold, New Jersey. The next season I worked with Pastor Dexter Polnitz at Great Day Ministries in East Hampton, New Jersey, as the Pastor's secretary and evangelist in training under their doctrine, now located in Cherry Hill, New Jersey. My season was up and I continued to do God's work from home with Pastor Andru Kelly, founder, president, and CEO of One Church Worldwide Ministries (Hour of Power) Teleconference along with the Inner-Core, as we are intercessors for the Lord to go (God's mandate) and reach the lost souls for Christ. We intended to show love and encourage all of God's people. Now I'm waiting for my next mission, for this season has ended. I love reaching God's people.

LONNEICE WEEKS-BADLEY

NOTE FROM THE EDITOR

Lonneice Badley has a winning way with words. Her poetry is inspirational and accessible, full of raw emotion and deep faith, and her message is clear: We must focus on God to win the spiritual battle being waged in our minds.

"OP" THE AWARD OF APPRECIATION

OutSkirts Press and Team Leaders you're the best. No way! I will not close this book without given my heart felt gratitude and appreciation you all for a great job, and I say well done.

You all deserve special acknowledgements for it surely was a "great adventure" you helped me to present these writes (Mind Games) to the eyes of others and to the market place and yes! We worked together as a winning team.

The "OP" Team Leaders that encouraged me are:

Tina Ruvalcaba-*Publishing Consultant*, Lisa Buckley-*Author Representative*, Barbara Crain-I*mage Review Specialist and the Production team*.

To My readers or writers if you know of someone or maybe you are looking for a winning team I recommend "OP" and the complete team leaders. Use the info below freely and when you do; you will agree that this "OP" Team will lead you to a new life as an Author/Writer or Self Publisher. You will be searched out as one; everyone would love to see; how great your writes would be and they would be anxious to read, read, and read and pass it forward as my facebook friend and Author/Writer Eric L. Burt - Inside the Soul of Me; passed it forward to me.

Outskirts Press, Inc.
10940 S. Parker Road - 515
Parker, CO 80134
1.888.OP.BOOKS ext. 756
1.888.208.8601 – Fax
www.outskirtspress.com

May God Bless each and every one of you today and forever...
One Love
Lonneice Weeks-Badley

CPSIA information can be obtained at www.ICGtesting.com
Printed in the USA
BVOW080343141212

308121BV00004B/56/P

9 781432 798222